A
Metamorphosis
of the Soul

Lessons from my journey on faith,
hope, love and perseverance

C J Brown

WESTBOW
PRESS
A DIVISION OF THOMAS NELSON
& ZONDERVAN

Scripture taken from the King James Version of the Bible.

Scripture quotations taken from the New American Standard Bible®, Copyright © 1960, 1962, 1963, 1968, 1971, 1972, 1973, 1975, 1977, 1995 by The Lockman Foundation. Used by permission." (www.Lockman.org)

Unless otherwise noted in text, scripture reference is taken from the King James Version of the Bible.

WestBow Press books may be ordered through booksellers or by contacting:

WestBow Press
A Division of Thomas Nelson & Zondervan
1663 Liberty Drive
Bloomington, IN 47403
www.westbowpress.com
1 (866) 928-1240

Cover design created by Phillip J. Brown
Image page 15 © C. J. Brown

ISBN: 978-1-4908-2249-5 (sc)
ISBN: 978-1-4908-2250-1 (hc)
ISBN: 978-1-4908-2248-8 (e)

Library of Congress Control Number: 2014900698

Printed in the United States of America.

WestBow Press rev. date: 01/21/2014

Contents

For my mother and grandmothers, who
are always with me in spirit.

Acknowledgments

A Metamorphosis of the Soul is the result of more than a half century of living, growing, and discovering the true essence of my soul. This book shares life changing experiences that touched my soul and positively transformed the way I saw and reacted to the world around me. These transformational experiences have been orchestrated by souls who have touched my life, serving as conductors and sentinels on this journey we call life.

At various intervals in life, we all experience reflective moments in which we consider the ups and downs and the joys and pains of simply living. Over the past five years especially, I have experienced exhilarating highs and dark lows along the way. This extreme dichotomy of experiences inspired me to document them through my writings. An awareness and assessment of those darkest and brightest moments has aided me in assessing their impact upon my life, and my spiritual growth.

I thank my lifelong childhood friends – Carr, Bev and others, who have been just that, friends who remembered to call on holidays when we were raising young families and cooking in small kitchens, trying to remember family recipes.

I thank those souls who have traveled with me partially or fully on this journey. They include my parents, grandparents, aunts, uncles, stepparents, siblings and colleagues. There are college friends – Syvil and Cornita, who have been with me since early adulthood and offered the best of themselves in friendship. No matter what city we have lived in, we have made the long distance calls, emailed or sent text messages to reminisce, offer love and support, and to remind ourselves that we'd always be there for each other.

To Rev. Dr. Clarence H. Burke, I thank you for the spiritual guidance that you have given me as I contemplated publication of this book. You have always been a source of spiritual guidance and support for my family regardless of my church affiliation. Your photography and your kind and quiet ways have been a true inspiration. Thank you for letting God work through you in such a blessed way.

To my husband Phillip, I simply say "thank you" for your quiet and undying love, our wonderful peaks and our darkest valleys, for without it all our love would be superficial and untested. Still waters do run deep and are ideal waters for divine anchors to rest in and keep us steady.

To David, Phillip, Jr. and Jennifer (our children), I thank God for allowing me to be a steward of your lives for a moment in time. I realize that you are not mine but God's. The joys and the challenges of being your parent are at the heart of many of my life experiences. I hope and pray that all I have attempted to teach you, all the values I have attempted to instill in you, and all the love that I gave of myself to you will serve as moral and spiritual compasses that will guide you through life, while I am here with you and when I am long departed.

I acknowledge my pastor Rev. Wayne A. Johnson, Sr., his wife, and the St. Stephen A.M.E. Church family for the spiritual home that St. Stephen has provided my paternal family for five generations. I am particularly grateful to the many teachers who came through St. Stephen over the years and who served as my academic conductors and sentinels on the journey of life. People such as Ruthy R. Davis, Katie B. Foreman, Mamie Harris, Louvenia Sneed and Melvin Thompson grounded me. They instilled within me a strong sense of self-esteem during segregation and desegregation of public schools in the south. I will always remember the transforming effect upon me and other classmates when we watched our third grade teacher, Mrs. Katie B. Foreman, cry outside our classroom door at the news of President Kennedy's assassination. Also within my church family I take this opportunity to express my gratitude to Mr. Alexander Sloan, Jr. and the Sloan family. My many childhood visits to the Sloan home will always invoke fond memories. I effortlessly recall playing the Bible Game with Sheila over peanut butter and jelly sandwiches. My deep relational roots with other St. Stephen families since childhood have been just as important in various ways. Thank you for sowing good seeds so early in my life.

Most importantly, I thank GOD for allowing me to live long enough to begin to tell my story. I am grateful for the mountains and the valleys that He has brought me over and through, for they remind me of the source of my strength and the reason for my joy. I thank Him for responding to my prayers for discernment and spiritual wisdom as I attempted to find my way and walk closer with Him. I thank Him for teaching me the beauty of giving so that I could receive; praising so that I would be blessed; and having compassion so that He would show compassion to me. As He has answered my many prayers and allowed His light to shine on my path, my steps have been realigned and ordered in His will. What joy it gives the soul when you realize His will, submit, and enjoy His benefits! Only He could be exalted in the most exhilarating moments of my life and only He has sustained me in my darkest moments of life, giving me peace beyond any understanding and bestowing benefits upon me that my soul could never understand by worldly standards.

It is my hope that this text will be an inspiration to other souls finding their way on the journey we call life.

"I will bless the LORD at all times: his praise
shall continually be in my mouth."
(Psalm 34:1)

Introduction

This experience called life is a journey. Some believe that what we experience in the 'here and now' is it, and that nothing else follows. I and many others believe that this portion of the journey is what we call 'life' and that there is more to the journey after 'this life'. The more we learn about this journey, and the expectations of our Creator, the more successful we can be on our way.

Our spiritual infancy and youth are characterized by very human traits of dependency, worldliness, and a general lack of awareness of our true spiritual selves. It is a delicate time in the course of life, for with proper nurturing, our souls will grow and mature into the beautifully unique beings that we were created to be. As a result, we are empowered and anointed to productively engage with other souls, to live more fruitful lives, and to be more wholesome individuals, living harmoniously and productively within our communities. A void or an imbalance in this process leads to a life that falls short of God's will for us and becomes fertile ground for unfulfilled hopes and dreams, and discontent souls. The divine spark in each of us mandates an ongoing transformation or metamorphosis of our souls. Only through this transformation can we fully realize who we are and how we can live the best lives God intends for us to have.

For this reason, I have written and offer this book as a glimpse into the joys, disappointments and general experiences of life that have transformed my soul. Each section of this book offers reflections, scripture, and opportunities for you, the reader, to make life applications to your own spiritual journey. As this manuscript developed, I realized many parallels between my own spiritual development and the life cycle of butterflies, thus the title *A Metamorphosis of the Soul*.

The butterfly has four primary life cycles. In its earliest stage of development, butterfly eggs are laid by the adult female in a fertile and safe plant environment. This enables the young, newly hatched butterfly to have a nourishing and sustaining food source as it grows. Consider what happens in the earliest stages of our lives. Our parents place us in nurturing and safe environments. Whatever we consume for our bodies or our souls is designed to be good for us. We are shielded from anything considered detrimental to our growth and well-being. As we grow, we consume, and we consume at a very rapid pace. We observe, we consume, we digest and we mimic. Our environment plays a tremendous role in who we become. The food we eat impacts our physical growth and our overall health, just as our experiences with others shape our view of the world and how we should interact with one another. Much like butterflies in the caterpillar stage, we continue to consume, consume, consume. Unlike the caterpillar, we do not have a good defense mechanism and become susceptible to predatory situations that can affect or deter our growth and development.

As we begin to develop mature personality traits, our character develops and we seek deeper meaning and understanding of our life journey. Similar to butterflies in the pupa stage, we attach ourselves to a support system. That system can surround us, encase us, and serve as protection for us as we transform into the beautiful spiritual beings that we were designed to be. Whether through our church affiliations, scholarly studies, independent self-reflection or peer groups, we begin a most critical phase of our transformation from the immature soul to the mature soul – a transformation that can occur multiple times before we are molded into our true selves.

For butterflies, this stage of metamorphosis, *or transformation*, is critical and success depends in part on how well they are insulated or shielded from interference with the growth process. The fully grown caterpillar (pupa) enters a hard outer shell known as a *chrysalis*, which protects it from interference as it transforms into a mature butterfly. Inside the chrysalis, the transformation from a dependent, consuming, 'infant' occurs to transform the immature being into the mature and beautiful butterfly. In church we sing hymns and study scripture about this stage of our spiritual growth. The sixth chapter of the book of Ephesians offers my most favorite writings about going forth with the full protection of God.

In church, we liken this stage of our development to being placed on the potter's wheel and reshaped or like being burnished in the heat of a divine flame. The anatomical structure of the caterpillar in this stage is broken down and reshaped then replaced with the structure that will emerge as a butterfly. For humans our transformation from worldly to spiritually mature, while under the nurturing protection of our churches, our studies, and our God, cause us to emerge anew, transformed in spirit and heart. We emerge with a deeper understanding of our purpose, God's will and our calling in life. For the adult butterfly, it emerges from its protective case when it is fully mature. In our case, we emerge reshaped and transformed but never veering far from our protection since our transformation is ongoing.

This is the analogy to my own spiritual growth. I was born, raised and nurtured in an environment designed to develop me both physically and spiritually. Environmental influences played a role but as I emerged, the process repeated itself through several cycles and events in my life – each one causing me to experience a deeper maturation of my soul. I imagine the process continues throughout life's entire journey for would we not want learning and growth to be a lifelong experience?

In this book, I share with you just a few of the transforming events that began in my childhood and continued into my adulthood. Each round of transformation has taken me higher and higher, deeper and deeper in my relationship with God. Because I am a Christian by baptism and profession of faith, I speak to you through my writings about God and our relationship with Him.

I am not a minister, nor am I a theologian. However, I attempt to share with you my perspectives as a woman of faith, tempered with God's word as received from Scripture. I give honor to God for His presence in my life, all the days of my life. In an era when we are besieged with broken relationships, government turmoil, depression, mental illness, violence, poverty and so many other social ills, *A Metamorphosis of the Soul* provides encouragement and inspiration to those seeking peace, harmony and ongoing spiritual growth. It is my hope that you will be inspired to reflect upon your own journey through life and consider the metamorphosis of your soul.

Part I

Stepping Stones

Experts have offered many opinions and writings about spiritual growth and the stepping stones to developing a mature soul. The following principles have guided my journey and establish the foundation for this book.

BELIEF
Acceptance of who we are as spiritual beings

FAITH and TRUST
Realization that without an effective, individual relationship with God we will never realize our full potential

PRAYER
The ongoing conversation that we must have with God

OBEDIENCE and SUBMISSION
Compliance with God's will for our lives

REPENTANCE and FORGIVENESS
Ongoing repentance when we live outside of His will

LOVE
The most important principle, which if absent leaves us devoid of the greatest of all gifts

"A good name is rather to be chosen than great riches, and loving favour rather than silver and gold."
(Proverbs 22:1)

What's In a Name?

When I was a child my mother and aunts often told me stories of my godmother, Elfenia. She was one of my mother's dear friends and was named godmother to me and my brother in part because of her role in naming me when I was born. Apparently, Mary was the chosen name. I guess Mary would've been just fine as it's biblical, and I like biblical names. But I didn't have a say in the matter.

My godmother's decision on Cynthia, as I was told, was because the name has Greek origins. In her opinion with a common surname of Brown, I needed a more 'worldly' first name. As the story was told to me, my godmother's hope was that I would get a good education, do well in life, but most importantly develop an awareness and appreciation for other people and cultures of the world. In her mind, Cynthia would be a name that would somehow expand my outlook on life.

As a young child, there was no Internet, PBS station, or *Sesame Street* broadcasting into our home. Growing up in a small Southern town, there were only two primary television stations, along with radio. Beyond school, community and church experiences in the segregated South, my parents, my godmother and my aunts exposed us to the world outside of our community with trips (both inside and out of the state), *National Geographic* and a myriad of other magazines, and the best reference books I could have imagined at that time, *World Book* encyclopedias. I think everyone had them or *Encyclopedia Britannica*. In addition, my godmother made sure we had the yearbooks and the special supplements and she would even stop by occasionally and test us on everything from NASA missions to African tribes.

I occasionally reflect on those days with a little humor but realize she was attempting to instill something beyond the ordinary in me. My godmother's hope for me to be aware of and sensitive to other people and cultures was realized. Her influence in my life was a part of the nurturing that would shape who I became as an adult as she somehow instilled in me an appreciation for diversity and culture.

She was not, however, the only woman who influenced my spiritual and cultural growth beyond my mother and my grandmothers. My grandmother's cousin Nada always pointed out a second or third book about other cultures and people when I made my weekly trips to the "colored" library as a child. Pages from *"Christmas Around the World"* and other books that exposed me to worlds beyond my neighborhood are still vivid in my mind. My childhood birthday and Christmas gifts of books from my aunt Dorothy (now a retired children's librarian) influenced my appreciation for the printed word. I now understand why my mother vehemently resisted my father's desires for me to attend white segregated schools in my hometown that were being integrated during the integration of public schools. The educators and leaders in the neighborhood schools I attended instilled a sense of pride and drive in me that I don't believe I would have received elsewhere in that particular era. My father's family history in the administration of Peabody School and my mother's friendships with elementary and middle-grade teachers at both Peabody and Dudley schools gave me a stern sense of discipline and security during this time. Simultaneously, my character was being molded by informed and intelligent people from my own community who didn't just teach academics but taught culture, social skills and pride to a young African American girl growing up in a tumultuous time in American history. Watching my third-grade teacher and one of her colleagues crying outside the classroom door on the day of President John F. Kennedy's assassination was yet another transforming experience that being a third-grader in Peabody School afforded me. The experience helped build my character, even as a young girl; the experience caused an early metamorphosis of my soul.

As the years passed, my stepmother Vera gave me love, care, and insight when I was a rebellious teenager. She quelled my anger with my parents, and helped me to know myself. In the sixties when everyone donned their Afros and dashikis, my mother insisted that I be mainstream in appearance and behavior. But it was my stepmother who bought my first dashiki and encouraged my Afro hairdo. I remember returning home after a Thanksgiving visit with my father and stepmother.

When I went to school on that Monday, some of the boys in class made fun of my new Afro. My teenage nickname -C.B.- was not for my initials. It was because the boys thought my head looked like a cedar bush, and they couldn't believe I had traded in my press 'n' curl hairdo for an Angela Davis look. The peer pressure didn't work. I was ridiculed that entire school year. Yet my soul was being transformed, and I was developing the self-confidence I would need in years to come.

Despite my godmother's opinion about my name, I once read that the name Cynthia was the name given by the ancient Greeks to their moon goddess. Although I am mono-theistic and Christian in faith, I do believe the name Cynthia is relevant to my journey. My ongoing thirst for knowledge, not just for my own sake but to shed light on situations, may in fact be personified in my name.

My name is Cynthia, and I am proud of who Cynthia is. The women in my life loved, nurtured, and protected me enough, to build my self-esteem and help me to have a reasonable portion of self-confidence rather than arrogance. They are not all named here, but they touched my soul in my earliest, formative years. My roots have kept me grounded and helped me to understand the beauty and importance in knowing and loving myself. I have grown to realize that you cannot effectively love others unless you first love yourself. I have also learned to be confident in who you are, be knowledgeable of the stock from which you come, and to stand your ground on that which you know to be true and right even when at a very high price.

My name is Cynthia, and I am grateful for the divine and ongoing transformations of my soul.

Reflections
Have you ever considered the meaning of your name?
Do you believe that your name personifies
your personality or character?
What evidence have you seen of this?

"Ye are the light of the world. A city that is set on an
hill cannot be hid. Neither do men light a candle,
and put it under a bushel, but on a candlestick; and
it giveth light unto all that are in the house. Let your
light so shine before men, that they may see your good
works, and glorify your Father which is in heaven."

(Matthew 5: 14- 16)

Go to the Garden Alone

As a very young child, I grew up in the Baptist Church, the denomination of my mother's parents. My grandmother was an invalid, due to a lifelong heart ailment, so by the time of my birth, attending church regularly was not an option for her. My mother taught school outside of the county in which we lived and traveled back and forth during the week. My father also taught school and was away in the summers playing baseball on the Negro League circuit. By the time I was three or four years old, he was away in the fall studying at Howard University School of Medicine. My grandfather worked for the Atlantic Coast Line Railroad and made weekly runs as far south as Jacksonville, Florida, and as far north as Richmond, Virginia. I therefore spent many hours with my grandmother and the lady who came in to help at the house, Miss Minnie.

I have fond and vivid memories of bringing the newspaper in from the front porch for my grandmother to read each day. Aside from my parents, she was my first teacher, teaching me phonics as I learned to sound out the headlines of the daily newspaper at age three. I also have my memories of Shiloh Missionary Baptist Church in my hometown, Sunday school, and Vacation Bible School lessons. My grandmother would teach me songs for Sunday school even before I could read well. One hymn was an old family favorite: "I Come to the Garden Alone".

This hymn had a special meaning to us because in spite of her infirmities, my grandmother always mustered the strength to work in her flower garden. I grew from a toddler to kindergartener to elementary school student anticipating the colors of spring, summer, and fall in her garden each year. There were dahlias, zinnias, daisies and my favorite, black-eyed Susans. There were other favorites that grew like bushes, hydrangea, oleander, and gardenias. Her apple tree always bore beautiful blossoms, and her crepe myrtle trees graced us with an abundance of pink and white blossoms. She grew the most beautiful yellow, pink and red roses that I've ever seen outside of a florist shop. Even as an adult, I have not cultivated roses like my grandmother's, although I try. Standing stately, outside of our little home were two live oak trees, a reminder of the strength of deep roots and perseverance - attributes of strong families and their values.

I attribute my love of nature, and especially plants and flowers to my maternal grandmother. Somehow even my fear of creeping creatures such as worms or slugs was alleviated by her. At the first sign of a pest, she would send my aunt to buy a small can of beer and pour a bit in saucers for placement throughout the garden. Magically, the pesky little creatures would be dead the next morning – I only imagine drowned in their own drunken stupor. It worked! She always reminded me that a good gardener must be vigilant against pests that will rob the garden of its beauty.

Although she was not physically able to use garden tools like the hoe or the rake, she would bend and pull weeds occasionally. I would follow behind her, the curious little student, with a paper bag for her to dump them in, for pulling them and leaving them on the dirt only gave an opportunity for the weeds to somehow take root again. Nana's advice was that weeds will always get into the garden, so you must pull them before they take root and gain a stronghold. If that happened it would require more effort to get them out, and you ran the risk of them damaging the roots of your flowers and them choking them to death. I would learn the value of this lesson many years later in my career.

As an adult I began to make the same analogy to life situations. I would call upon my grandmother's simple wisdom to help me through difficult moments in life. Whether in the garden, at work, church, personal matters or serving the community, weeds can take hold and wreak havoc. I began to refer to weeds as the acronym for destructive forces

Whether in the garden, at work, church, personal matters or serving the community, weeds can take hold and wreak havoc. I began to refer to weeds as the acronym for destructive forces I would encounter; those people or situations that **W**illfully, **E**ncourage or **E**xecute **D**amage for **S**elf-gratification.

I would encounter; those people or situations that **W**illfully, **E**ncourage or **E**xecute **D**amage for **S**elf-gratification. On my journey I would find that my grandmother was right. If you don't pull weeds before they take root, removal can require much labor, effort, and time. If you are not careful the weeds can damage, even destroy the roots of your most beautiful flowers, ultimately destroying the garden.

I learned another invaluable lesson from her about the garden. Sometimes when I would kneel to help her plant seeds in the spring, she would talk with me about the importance of praying. As a child I did not realize the depth of her messages about prayer. At best, I memorized verses such as *Now I lay me down to sleep, I pray the Lord my soul to keep, If I should die before I wake, I pray the Lord my soul will take.* By kindergarten it was the Lord's Prayer and before she passed away, when I was in elementary school, it was Psalm 23. Her words to me about prayer and meditation were simple, but it would be many years before the gravity of her words would make a full impact on my soul. What I understood most as a child was her assurance that some of our best conversations with God can occur in the quiet of the garden and in the midst of the beauty God gives us. She gave me tools to aid in the metamorphosis of my soul.

Go to the garden alone while the dew is still on the roses.
God will hear your prayers, He will show
He cares, Just put your trust in him.

Reflections

How have you protected the garden of your life?

Is it always easy to identify the weeds from the flowers?

When you find weeds in your garden, do you take care
to remove them before they develop strong roots?

Kindness Isn't a Gesture, It's a Trait

Kindness, a primary yield of love, seems to be in such high demand yet low quantity these days. We periodically hear or read news stories about random acts of kindness, but the individual sparks have not created their own bonfires. Hate crimes, institutional and systemic policies that breed racism, sexism and economic oppression still exist throughout the world. People have become increasingly cruel to one another. Respect for human life and simple expressions of kindness are rapidly disappearing in society. A smile as you pass someone in public, a kind gesture to a stranger, a basic "good morning" when you see a co-worker are becoming uncommon gestures in an almost hostile world.

My first job after college graduation was in a Goodwill Industries Rehabilitation facility. Despite a job offer that would allow me to launch my career in a different profession, I was led to accept a position that would keep me closer to home. This was not at all in my plans, but I wasn't feeling adventurous enough to live several states away. It was also a position that would allow me to learn more about helping the unemployed obtain gainful employment. It was the first step in developing my career that did not fit with my plans. I would later learn that it was not about my plan, but the divine plan for my life.

During my ten months on the job I worked with individuals who were injured at work and required rehabilitation to return to their trade. A particular gentleman on my caseload was a journeyman electrician who accidentally received a high voltage shock while working. Despite a minor physical disfiguration, he survived the accident. The emotional scar left by the accident prohibited him from returning to work in a highly paid trade. Of all the individuals I worked with that winter, he was the most difficult to reach. I sensed he did not feel that a young 21 year old African American woman could relate to his perspectives about life, work and his injury. It took several weeks of simple acts of kindness to break through the barriers between us. On some days, a kind gesture or word did not even receive a kind response from him. Yet week after week, I continued to chip away at the blank stares, the one word responses to questions, and the lack of engagement when we attempted to set plans for his ongoing rehabilitation. I simply returned disengagement with outreach and blank stares with smiles. I decided I could not quit although some days were difficult to say the least. It would have been easy to ask my supervisor for a different client and to have him removed from my caseload. However his livelihood was at stake, and he had a 90% chance for complete recovery and return to a lucrative job. I felt compelled to help him find his way forward.

I am not sure what the game changer was but by early spring, some 4 months after beginning my work with him, the kindness was reciprocated. After the winter of our relationship, he began to open up like daffodils breaking through once frozen ground. In the weeks to come, he would receive an offer to return to work with a major power company at what seemed to be an unbelievable salary with benefits. I was very pleased with his progress and his return to work, but never felt absolutely confident that anything I did really made a difference in his breakthrough. What mattered most was that the breakthrough occurred.

On his last day with us, he presented me with a ceramic candy dish. It sat on a small pedestal and inside the upper bowl of the dish was inscribed the words "Good Luck" with a horseshoe and pink flowers. When he gave me the dish, I was speechless. As I admired the beauty of the craftsmanship I asked him who made it. He explained that he made it for me in appreciation for my unrelenting spirit to draw him out of the dark place he had gone to after his accident. An older man, at least twice my age, he explained his upbringing and his beliefs, and that in fact he initially resented having me assigned as his coordinator. My initial instincts were right. He didn't feel that there was anything I could do, as a woman, or as an African-American to help him. However the fact that I didn't return his bitterness with more bitterness broke the negativity he was feeling.

He went on to explain that making pottery was one of his hobbies. After his accident, he had abandoned it and many other simple pleasures in life. The candy dish was his first product from the potter's wheel in a very long time.

I received that gift 35 years ago. It has traveled with me to the few offices that I have worked in over the span of my career. Each time I look at it, I am reminded that the various forms of negativity in our world will never be defeated with more of the same. Simple acts of kindness, that burn into a bonfire will stave off the negative and bring forth the positive. I am also reminded to smile, even when the load is heavy and the sky is gray.

> Simple acts of kindness, that burn into a bonfire will stave off the negative and bring forth the positive. I am also reminded to smile, even when the load is heavy and the sky is gray.

Over the years, I have received small but powerful gifts from co-workers and other individuals whom I have helped through my work. One plaque reads "Rise by Lifting Others"; another reads "It is in giving that we receive". A favorite that hung on my wall for many years reads:

"People love underdogs but like to follow top dogs…
Follow some underdogs anyway
People will attack you if you try to help them
But help them anyway
People will claim you have selfish, ulterior
motives when you try to do good
DO GOOD ANYWAY

If you get kicked in the butt for giving your best
Keep giving your best anyway
Don't gloat on the good you do now; it will
most likely be forgotten tomorrow
But keep doing good anyway
Years will be spent building up good things
that others will tear down overnight
But keep building because in the end
It's all between you and God, not you and them."

My experience affirmed my beliefs. I still have my candy
dish and the wall hangings given to me over the years.

Reflections
When was the last time you were met with adversity
that prevented you from completing a task?
How did you respond to it?
Did you feel stronger or weaker after the experience?
How will you use the experience to generate
more positive energy in others?

"Do not let kindness and truth leave you; bind them around your neck, write them on the tablet of your heart."

(Proverbs 3:3, NASB)

"Two are better than one; because they have a good reward for their labour. For if they fall, the one will lift up his fellow: but woe to him that is alone when he falleth; for he hath not another to help him up."

(Ecclesiastes 4:9-10)

Two are Better than One

I recently watched a morning news cast about a young woman on vacation who suffered a freak accident causing her to lose one of her legs. As the story unfolded, I learned that the woman was enjoying a visit with her "best friend". While out sight-seeing and without warning a vehicle ploughed into her pathway. As she explained, she couldn't move in any direction to avoid being hit. Lying on the pavement injured and bleeding profusely, total strangers came to her rescue. A tourniquet applied by one of the strangers reportedly saved her life. The woman was far from home and recalled wanting her mother by her side as she was being rushed to the hospital. The presence of her best friend brought relief that she had difficulty expressing in words. The depth of their friendship beamed from their faces into the camera.

In spite of this devastating incident she attributed the presence of her best friend to her recovery from the amputation, but most importantly to her positive outlook on the entire situation. The woman and her friend were wearing pink and green dresses, respectively. Seeing them reminded me of the love and care of one of my dearest friends in life.

Syvil and I met in college, "line sisters" on an uncommon line of two. We were pledging Alpha Kappa Alpha Sorority, Inc. Our pledge experience was a good one – nothing at all like the hazing stories you read or hear of in some organizations and at some college campuses. Instead it was one of learning, growing and bonding. Once, when a member of the sorority made a sharply critical comment to Syvil I recall becoming defensive and protective of her to the point of considering dropping from the process. On the day of our induction, our advisor pulled me to the side with a smile on her face and explained that the comments that upset us were intentionally made to help us bond. She reminded us that once we left the protected halls of academia, we would enter into a world that can be cruel and challenging. She further reminded me that if we were sincere about the process and not just trying to affiliate with the organization for superficial reasons, the bond we developed during the pledge experience would carry us throughout life and help us to be strong, one for the other. She was right, and I didn't fully understand how right she was until many years later.

We were both women from "salt of the earth" families. My sister was many years younger so during my early adulthood Syvil filled the void of not having a sister close by and of relatively close age. We both understood the responsibilities of being the eldest sibling and the expectations associated with that status. That sense of responsibility carried over into the deepening of our friendship.

Shortly after graduation she and her husband moved away to begin their careers. I was in the early years of a human resource management career, also with a very young family but remained in the Research Triangle Park area of the state. A short time after, Syvil and her family returned to the area (which was her home) to fully launch their careers. We didn't see each other daily as we did in college, but our relationship grew to the truest extent of friendship. We would reminisce and laugh about learning to step to Earth, Wind and Fire tunes in college. We shared recipes and discussed ways to save and budget with young and growing families. Realizing that life was no longer about "us" as college coeds, Syvil taught me all of the outlet mall shopping tips to ensure the right look at the right price. Even when I couldn't master the budget to ensure an annual vacation every year, Syvil and her husband perfected their budgeting to ensure an annual skiing trip for their young family. By the time she "taught" me the right budget tips for the big annual vacation we were exchanging notes on international travel.

One afternoon following a full and exhausting day at work, I found myself in a situation that proved to be life changing and transforming. I became a victim of domestic violence and it changed the course of my personal life. My young son was fortunately, spending a week with his grandparents a few hours away when it happened. What lasted for minutes seemed like hours and when it was over my escape from it all was to seek refuge at a neighborhood police station. Domestic violence had not yet come to the forefront of social priorities for policy makers so upon my arrival at the neighborhood police station. I was politely told by the desk officer to try to "work it out" because there was nothing he could do. Battered and defeated, I walked the many blocks back to my home. I still don't know why I didn't just drive my car in the beginning, but in a strange way the walk was therapeutic. Along the way, I could only imagine the disbelief and anger that my parents and family would have felt if they were aware of the incident. I thanked God that my son was with his grandparents and not present to witness something so unimaginable and so violent.

When I arrived home, I was relieved to find an empty house. Tired and sweaty from the long walk home, and with a swollen face and ringing ears, I collapsed on the floor of the master bedroom. The soft carpet on the floor cushioned my fall. All I could do was pray a prayer of thanksgiving for being alive, for not allowing the incident to drive me to do something crazy, and to pray for help. I was too tired and too injured to even call home to my mother or to think about seeking medical attention. I simply curled up and fell asleep on the floor.

At some point in the night, I heard a voice asking "are you alright?" I don't recall responding or even moving. What I do know though is that God answered my prayer for help because the next voice I heard spoke softly to me saying "CB, CB, are you ok? Get up…". It was Syvil. When I did not report for work the next day, she was the person who came to find me. She took me to the hospital to receive medical attention and stayed with me throughout the process. We talked about what happened and how I should proceed, but she allowed me the space to make my own decisions. Little did either of us know that her submission to God's divine influence early in her life had given her a level of wisdom that I had yet to experience and grow in to. Although she was a few years younger than I, for years to come she would keep me on her spiritual radar, almost as an older sister keeps watch over a younger sister.

In the years that followed, we both pursued other life goals and raised our families (and in my case divorced and later remarried the man who proved to be my true soul mate). The bond established through the sorority brought us together. But the *substance* of our relationship, not our membership in the organization, defined our true friendship. It was the nurturing and growth of our individual relationship, one to the other, that simmered like homemade chicken soup on a cold winter day. It has been that chicken soup that has kept us for more than 30 years in a friendship that has never failed. Whether we agreed or disagreed, laughed or cried, we have always been there for each other. Actually, she has always been there for me… especially on birthdays when I missed a date by a day or two, yet, she never did.

The true mark of friendship was divinely placed upon us which is not the case in every relationship. I would come to learn that business and social relationships are not synonymous with true friendship. We often hope this higher level of relationship will manifest itself in lesser relationships but we must be ever mindful of the true nature of friendship. Friendships are not envious, vain or self-serving. Friends don't throw rocks and hide behind trees afterwards. Friends instead stand together

••••••••••❦••••••••••

I would come to learn that true friendships are precious and are few and far between. They are relationships that transcend all others except our relationship with God. Despite the numerous acquaintances we develop over time, it is those true friendships that help us along life's journey.

••••••••••⬆••••••••••

in times of adversity, standing the test of time and providing loving care and support for one another. I would come to learn that true friendships are precious and are few and far between. They are relationships that transcend all others except our relationship with God. Despite the numerous acquaintances we develop over time, it is those true friendships that help us along life's journey.

There would be other women aside from my female relatives who would help me find my way along the journey and nurture my soul. From finding peace in quilting to teaching me how to give unselfishly to those in need, they have proven to be the dearest of friends. They have added substance to each transformation of my soul and they have guided and supported me when the true meaning of the word friendship was tested. As my soul has transformed, I am grateful for the spiritual lessons I have learned on the journey about discerning true friends from acquaintances.

Reflections

What has been one of the darkest moments in your life?
Did you have a friend to help you confront it?
Where is your friend now, and do you
maintain contact with him or her?
How has your friend helped you to realize that he
or she is more than just an acquaintance?

Part II
Knowing That You're Growing

"I beseech you therefore, brethren, by the mercies of
God, that ye present your bodies a living sacrifice, holy
acceptable unto God, which is your reasonable service.
And be not conformed to this world: but be ye transformed
by the renewing of your mind, that ye may prove what
is that good, and acceptable, and perfect, will of God.
For I say, through the grace given unto me, to every man
that is among you, not to think of himself more highly
than he ought to think; but to think soberly, according
as God hath dealt to every man the measure of faith."
(Romans 12: 1-4)

Looking in the Mirror

Many years ago, while working for then Illinois Bell/Ameritech Corporation, my colleagues and I underwent customer service training. The extensive program was designed to help us represent the corporation effectively, maximize customer satisfaction through excellent customer service, and help us to fine-tune our customer service skills so that we were constantly aware of our image as an Ameritech leader. Such training and development activities were vital to the success of the corporation – both in bottom-line profits and overall corporate image.

One segment of the training involved understanding ourselves as managers so that we were approachable in the eyes of our customers. This segment included a component which I recall as the "360 degree look in the mirror". The goal was to see ourselves through our own eyes, but to understand how others "see" us, and in turn to find the best balance between our self-perception and that of others. An inability to reach this goal meant failure in building customer relationships. There were of course, all types of leadership tests administered to us such as the Meyers-Briggs. However they only provided a limited perspective on our style as managers. The "look in the mirror" caused us to examine ourselves in a deeper sense. Sometimes surprising, sometimes confirming, and sometimes even painful, the results caused us to emerge from the exercise more sensitive to our individual style and how it affected our relationships with others. More importantly, we learned that a failure to constantly assess and reassess our style only hindered our relationships with potential customers. As our customer base evolved, it was critically important to assess ourselves on a regular basis.

This exercise is a critical one as we grow spiritually and our souls continue to transform. Just as I sought corporate acceptance and success in the business world, my transformed soul now seeks acceptance and success in my relationship with God through Christ. Do we look in the mirror only to see ourselves – approved by man and liked by the world? Or do we look in the mirror seeking an image that is Christ-like, not necessarily popular in the world but validated by scripture. It was an exercise and a lesson that I did not fully appreciate or learn well until many years after the Illinois Bell training. But it is a lesson well worth learning, for our souls cannot and will not transform if the standard is set by anything other than scripture. It is a difficult exercise to complete, but most importantly once you complete the assessment it is critical to fine tune what you see. It is an exercise that we must perpetually undergo to experience a positive transformation of our souls.

Reflections

It is so easy for us to have a myopic view of ourselves, others and life situations. Even in Christian seasons of self-denial and self-reflection, it is often difficult for us to "see" and acknowledge things as they really are. It is our self-serving and protective human nature that causes us to gravitate to the tangible rather than seeing the intangible. The soul is tested by life situations, but the victory is won when we acknowledge that it is not about us. Just as we often feel a need to help others transform and see beyond themselves, we too must be in a perpetual state of self-assessment. Without doing so, we risk failure in our efforts to grow and be more like Christ on our journey through life.

How do you self-assess to determine your effectiveness?
Do you look beyond the person you
see in the mirror each day?
What steps do you take to maintain an ongoing
sense of self-awareness and self-improvement?

"But whoso hath this world's good, and seeth his brother have need, and shutteth up his bowels of compassion from him, how dwelleth the love of God in him? My little children, let us not love in word, neither in tongue; but in deed and in truth."

(I John 3:17-18)

Care and Compassion for Others

It was the winter of 1989. I was living in Chicago and working downtown in the Loop. My office was a beautiful corner office in the old Illinois Bell headquarters building. Unlike the breathtaking Lake Michigan views that corporate executives had, I was located just a few floors above ground level with a view of the busy inner-workings of the Chicago business community. I was just far enough from ground level to have the hustle and bustle of street noises buffered, but close enough to see the people and the activity that make the city work.

On this particular day, my co-worker Terri and I contemplated our daily trek out for lunch. Although I was married with children, I was not always diligent about packing my lunch. I should've been to be thrifty, but also something that would save me a journey out into the cold and ice on a wintery day. There were food options available inside the building, but we were determined, almost driven, to venture out to a favorite salad bar to get a "healthy" lunch and trek back to the office. There was something that simply made no sense about it all, yet we justified it as going out to get some fresh air.

As we braved the Chicago wind walking the block or two that we had to travel, I noticed a silhouette of a person huddled in an alley. I paused for a moment but quickly picked up my pace when Terri called out "What's wrong? This wind is whippin' out here girl, hurry up". It was really cold that day and to help me along the way, I conjured memories of mild North Carolina winter days along the southeastern coast. Somehow my memories of home, so deeply present in my soul, broke the sting of the cold wind against my face.

After packing up our salads, having them weighed and preparing to take everything back to work (of course to eat as we perused the latest trade journals, or signed documents awaiting approvals on our desks), we braved the cold and headed back to headquarters. Keeping a pace almost as though marching to a military drum cadence, I glanced quickly as we passed the alley where earlier I thought I saw a person huddled in the cold. The body was gone. I thought perhaps I just imagined it, but the image wouldn't leave my mind that day.

A day later, after bringing lunch to work, I decided to take the trek outside in the cold in search of the mysterious silhouette. I didn't know who or what, I just knew that it was really cold outside and although panhandlers were common sights in the city, this person was not panhandling. He or she was just huddled down against the wall of a building. So I bundled up, got on the elevator and pushed the button for the first floor. Something in my conscious was saying "You're crazy... so what if you find someone huddled in that alley? Then what? You can't feed them, you can't take them home, and you can't get them a place to live. SO GO BACK UPSTAIRS OUT OF THE COLD, BACK TO YOUR GOOD TELECOMMUNICATIONS MANAGEMENT POSITION AND GET BACK TO WORK!" But a more serene and calm feeling immediately came over me and I felt that I must, so I walked out of the elevator when the door opened, and went in search of the mysterious silhouette.

Surely, it was not my imagination. There in the alley less than a block from my office, in about 15 degrees above zero temperature was a man. He sat on what appeared to be an old milk crate, huddled in a dark, worn overcoat. Remembering tips on safety from various training events, I immediately looked at his shoes (security classes taught us to be leery of panhandlers wearing new shoes or watches) but they were dirty, old and had ice caked around the edges of them.

As I stood before him I said a little prayer asking God to help me to help this person whom I didn't know, but felt a strong degree of empathy for. He looked up, an African-American man, appearing to be perhaps in his thirties. His eyes looked jaundiced and tired. There was nothing at all in his appearance that made me fearful. I naively asked him why he was outside huddled in the alley and didn't he have someplace to go. Slowly, he began to tell me that he had lost his job. His wife was sick and he had to take days off to take her to medical appointments for what ultimately proved to be a cancer diagnosis. When she could no longer work and the timeline for obtaining disability benefits became lengthy, they became delinquent in bills and ultimately were evicted from their rented home. She died and he struggled with whatever was left of their savings to bury her. He began to seek other employment and another steady place to live. But the missing piece that he couldn't explain well was that the ordeal left him with his own mental health challenges. Depression, despair, and mental fatigue had set in and he ended up in a shelter. The wind blew through the alley so hard that day. I stood against the wall to avoid being blown over while I listened. Something in me believed that he was telling the truth.

As he continued his story, he explained that he only had a few family members in the area but that they had their own challenges. He didn't want to live in an environment with them that would just further tax his soul. So until he could overcome his plight, he felt safer living in the cold during the day and the shelter at night.

I wanted to run. From our backyards, to our street corners to the full breadth of the world, poverty, homelessness and despair exist. We become immune to the harsh reality of it all. The real impact it has on our souls is frightening to most and to "protect" our spiritual selves from such situations we become callous. In that precise moment, the experience of empathy versus sympathy was overwhelming for me.

Less than a block away, I was in my warm comfortable office, working away in my corporate life, building my career. I took the train home to the suburbs every night (or my husband and I would drive in on days when the train schedule didn't match our need to be home early or make it to a school play or track meet at our children's schools). I didn't feel I had yet "arrived", but I was comfortable. I was living in the American mainstream. And although I knew of and saw poverty that exists in the city, and in my country, I had come face to face with it, up close and personal. It was a moment in time that transformed my soul.

There has and probably always will be a mindset in our modern culture that people in this predicament should just "pull themselves up by their boot straps". But the reality is that they can't always do so without help from someone. Remembering my safety tips, I had left my purse in my office and only left the building with my i.d. card, less than $20 in loose bills and keys. I wanted to offer him money but my conscious said *"offer him food"*. I did and he accepted but seemed embarrassed to walk into a restaurant, perhaps because of his appearance. So I trekked off to my lunchtime salad bar and purchased a sandwich and small salad. It was just one meal for one day but it was what I was compelled to do under the circumstances.

When I returned 15 minutes later he was still there. He thanked me and asked me why I did what I was doing. I simply said, "I don't know. Something made me come back after I saw you out here yesterday. It's so cold, I just couldn't believe you were out here in the cold like this." In his soft and weary voice he told me that he just hadn't been able to organize his thoughts and get moving to find programs that could help him. He sounded completely hopeless. I felt he probably was at a point of desperation that could have led him to just fall asleep on that crate one day and die in the cold.

In my spiritual infancy a divine spark of compassion burned within. Before her death, my mother always told me that I inherited this trait from her father, my maternal grandfather. My grandfather Ed, worked on the Atlantic Coast Line Railroad from the turn of the twentieth century until he retired well over 40 years later. His service was interrupted with a military stint in World War I but he resumed his railroad career after returning from the war. Although he was not a well educated man, he was an *intelligent* man and was very compassionate. My aunts and my mother would tell stories about his years working on the railroad during the Great Depression when he would return home at the end of a week on the rail with bags of rice, grits, flour and sugar for neighborhood families. It was the order of the day for him, and while he had his own vices, one of his greatest virtues was compassion for others.

Where I was so obsessed with career-building, raising children, and living in the American mainstream, I could not ignore the feeling that I experienced listening to this man in the alley and experiencing his plight. None of the service projects I had engaged in through my sorority or other organizations such as the Urban League or the Chicago-Cook County 4-H Foundation had invoked the feelings that I experienced on this day. I asked him to make his way back to the shelter and if it wasn't snowing to come back to the alley the next day. I wasn't sure if he would, but he said "OK".

My husband was employed at the time as an engineer for the University of Illinois. He occasionally worked odd hours and this was an evening when he was at work at the U of I

Medical Center. I didn't have him to talk to so after the children went to bed, I sat downstairs in the den with my dog after making a cup of tea, and had a little talk with God. I was still in a state of infancy in my relationship with God but we would meet sometimes over a cup of tea or coffee, in quiet places. This was one of those times. I didn't feel as though I received a clear answer to my questions about why I felt so sad about this person I had encountered. Neither did I feel as though I received a clear answer about what, if anything, I should or could do about it. After all, I could show up in the alley the next day and he might not even be there. I went to sleep hoping for an answer because I wasn't at ease. Sleep was and always has been therapeutic for me. True to form, I awoke the next morning with a clear charge.

After a full morning at work discussing college recruitment trips our team would travel out for, I marched out of my building at lunch time, wrapped in my down coat, hood and snow boots. Snow had fallen the night before and I didn't know if the mysterious man would still be there. After a good Chicago snow, the temperature always dropped and it got colder so I didn't know what to expect. But he was there, with his head bowed just as I saw him the first time. In my pocket was a neatly folded paper that I typed that morning with social programs listed. Earlier that day I called to find out how these outlets could help a person in his predicament and at least 2 or 3 committed to helping him if he would show up and ask for the contact person whose name I was given. I also had a C.T.A. bus pass for him and $20. I didn't know if this man would hock the bus pass for cash or use the money for liquor, beer or drugs.

My worldly senses cautioned me not to give this to him. My spiritual senses told me to get to that alley and do whatever I could to help. It seemed like so little, but with a tear running down his face from one eye, he said "Thank you Miss. No one has ever stopped to even ask me if I am OK. Thank you. I will go catch the bus right now."

I never saw that man again. We never even exchanged names. I don't know if he lived or died. It didn't matter. What mattered is that one soul attempted to help another soul in need without judgment or absolute validation of need. In the most basic and simple way help was offered and my steps were divinely ordered. I didn't talk with anyone about this except my colleague Terri, my husband, and my young children. Terri was an attorney so she of course had a critical and analytical mind. Both she and my husband cautioned me not to be a "bleeding heart" because there were too many people on the streets who were actually dangerous – either because of mental health issues or criminal mindsets. To an extent, they were right. But I was guided by a divine force which eased any reservations or fear that I experienced. So when the time came to act I stepped out on faith, without a word to anyone. I will never regret what I did nor the lesson that the experience taught me.

At the time, I didn't even know the proper way to relate the experience to scripture to help my children understand that we are our brother's keepers. My growth in better understanding and interpreting scripture was yet to come. It would be many years before I shared the experience with my children, and when I did it was to teach them two things. First, the smallest help is sometimes the greatest help. We should never discount any good deed that we can do for someone in need. Second, there is a divine lesson to learn in quietly doing for others without worldly recognition.

The experience transformed my soul. Helping others was no longer a matter of late night television commercials soliciting for donations. It was no longer akin to the multitude of mail solicitations that we all receive, especially during the holidays. It wasn't even the gratification of giving canned goods or back packs at church when giving in the community. Helping others became personal, and in my spiritual growth I came to realize that it's more than writing a check, making a donation or chatting about the plight of those in need over lunch with friends. I had to have an up close and personal experience with someone in need to move from sympathy to empathy. I realized that caring is not enough, compassion is what we all need to have more of. My soul was transforming. I would later learn that compassion would come at an even greater price in the ongoing transformation of my soul.

Reflections

When was the last time you did something for
someone without question or judgment?
Do you feel you make a greater impact when you help
others through a group effort or individually?
Why?

"Take heed that ye do not your alms before men, to be seen of them: otherwise ye have no reward of your Father which is in heaven. Therefore when thou doest thine alms, do not sound a trumpet before thee, as the hypocrites do in the synagogues and in the streets, that they may have glory of men. Verily I say unto you, They have their reward. But when thou doest alms, let not thy left hand know what thy right hand doeth: That thine alms may be in secret: and thy Father which seeth in secret himself shall reward thee openly."

(Matthew 6: 1 – 4)

The Color Orange

Of all the colors in the rainbow, I favor earth tones and hues that connect me with nature. Brown, green, beige, even muted shades of blue give me a feeling of peace and comfort. With clothing, I have always gravitated to black. It is not a favorite color for many, but one that I find unassuming and neutral. It is a color that I can coordinate virtually any other color in the rainbow with. Black always brings another color back into a sobering balance. It was not however, until I was almost 50 years old did I come to appreciate the color orange.

At the time I worked as a non-profit administrator. Since its inception, the organization where I was employed was rooted in a federal Head Start program. The agency had existed for 30 or more years before I was hired but during my tenure, the governing board of directors sought new opportunities to serve low-income families. One program that the agency began to administer was a federal Weatherization program. The overarching goal of the program was to assist low-income families through energy assessments of their dwellings and installation of energy efficient measures to reduce the energy burden on their household budgets. Simply put, home improvements to reduce energy bills for heating and cooling costs. Due to rapidly changing regulations, staff struggled with maintaining production levels and establishing a balance between customer expectations, regulatory requirements and funding source requirements. The work to be performed required our use of a subcontractor and even this posed challenges with training, again requiring compliance with multiple and sometimes conflicting demands from stakeholders.

This program was managed by an individual who reported to me. I periodically went on job sites to ensure customer satisfaction and to monitor progress and efficiency of projects. It was not the typical 'desk work' that I was accustomed to, but it was increasingly necessary as complaints rose and staff became frustrated.

On the particular day in mind, I visited the home of an elderly customer who had received energy efficiency services before our agency became the service provider in our area. The services received did not meet the current standards as taught in various training sessions for staff. After much discussion and negotiations, we were allowed by the funding source to provide services to the home but the work we were authorized to do was limited. Naturally, our customer didn't understand why.

Weatherization was not my area of expertise but I knew the lady needed help and above all else, she needed to understand what we could and couldn't do, and why. The manager was not successful in communicating with her so I went out to conduct the home visit myself. When I arrived at her house, I saw a beautiful array of tall orange flowers gracing the front entrance. Her garden was tiny, but the orange flowers made such a tremendous presence. Despite the fact that the house was old and desperately in need of repairs that we were not authorized to make, those flowers gave her house an almost regal stature.

The visit was difficult at best. I had to find the right ways to translate state and federal regulations into something that would be acceptable service in her mind. I also went prepared with a list of other programs that could complement the work our agency performed, but there was of course, the dreaded "waiting list" discussion that had to occur.

In the end, we concluded our meeting on a good note. She accepted all that I explained, and I vowed to walk with her through the next stages of obtaining service although it would not directly involve our agency. The lady was elderly, small, and frail at best. She offered me some tea at her small kitchen table. I declined, feeling she should keep all of her tea bags for a time when she might need them, given her fixed income. As we walked out of her front door, I began to compliment her on her garden and the beautiful orange flowers leaning towards her doorway.

In a delightful way she stopped me, and turned our conversation completely away from her home to the secret behind the beautiful orange flowers. "They're called 'Mexican Sunflowers. I grow them from seeds every year." We drifted off into a conversation about my grandmother, my childhood, and her flower garden. It was a good conversation on a late summer afternoon. When we finished I realized my husband was probably wondering why I was so late getting home because office hours were long over and pretty soon, the dinner hour would be over too.

She asked me to wait a minute but I told her I had to leave. I planned to make my report on her case the next day, then return later in the week to personally assist her in making contacts with other agencies for referral services. We had staff in the agency responsible for this but I felt an attachment to her after the visit and wanted to do it myself. She insisted that I wait, so I did.

After just a few minutes inside, she came back to the sidewalk where I had drifted ahead to. In her hand were two brown paper bags, each one larger than a school lunch bag but smaller than a grocery store bag. Smiling, she handed me the bags and said "Thank you for helping me. This is my gift to you for being so nice." I wasn't sure what was in the bags, so I smiled and with a bit of hesitation accepted them. Of course, my question was "What's in here?". Before I could peek in, she told me that they were the seeds for the beautiful orange flowers at her doorway. With an infectious grin, and a twinkle in her eyes she explained that every year she would harvest the seed balls from spent blossoms, and save them for next year's garden. Occasionally she would share with friends and/or neighbors although I didn't see any other yard on the block adorned with the beautiful orange blossoms.

She gave me a lesson on how to harvest the seeds each year, dry them in a paper bag over the winter, and plant in the spring. She assured me that each seed would yield a plant with multiple blooms, multiplying my seed harvest by 10 or 20 times over each year. She promised that the flowers would bring me more than just the enjoyment of the deep orange color that I so admired that day.

I didn't know what to say. "Thank you" didn't seem like nearly enough but in fact, it was. I also wasn't sure of what else the flowers might bring me beyond the visual enjoyment of color. They were not scented as a rose or lavender in the garden. But time was ticking away, and the sun was beginning to set so I said goodbye to her, bent over, and gave her a hug. I never saw her again because when I scheduled a return visit to help her with referrals, she was ill and ultimately a staff person returned to conduct the follow up.

The bags felt bulky so when I got in the car, I opened one of them to see what the seeds looked like. Not paying close attention, I stuck my finger on one of the prickly seed balls. The prick of my finger drew a little blood and brought to mind the sensation of a rose thorn. I looked carefully at the seed ball and wondered how something so dry and thorny could produce such a lovely and colorful flower.

Throughout the winter, I made sure to keep my brown paper bags in a cool and dry location. By the following spring, I carefully weeded the soil and reinforced it with nutrients to ensure fertile and fresh soil for the seeds to take root in. Through the months of May and June, I watched the seedlings grow to plants that were over five feet tall. By late July, buds began to appear and the show of orange swept through my garden.

By then, I had forgotten her closing words about the flowers bringing more than just the beautiful deep orange color. One Saturday afternoon while cleaning the kitchen, I looked out the window and across the deck. To my amazement, a parade of butterflies danced throughout the bed of Mexican Sunflowers. I had not seen that many butterflies since my childhood, at least not all at once and in a natural setting. They were beautiful and reminded me of childhood escapades, chasing the delicate and fluttering creatures in my grandmother's garden.

Stepping outside my role as an administrator and nurturing the human element in my interaction with another soul yielded a gift of immeasurable value. Compassion and kindness made all the difference that day. Each year, I harvest seeds from my Mexican Sunflowers and each year, I give a bag of seeds as a gift to someone. I've never stopped to study the botanical facts about the plant. I only know that they were given in appreciation, received with respect and gratitude, and as a result, the blossoms remind me each year of the goodness of giving of ourselves. That woman helped me on my journey of transformation and reminded me that everything we do for others cannot be measured by jobs, positions, or outcome reports. People sometimes just need to know that we care about one another.

Saving Hearts

"And I sent messengers unto them, saying, I am doing a
great work, so that I cannot come down: why should the
work cease, whilst I leave it, and come down to you?"
(Nehemiah 6: 3)

B oth of my parents suffered from forms of cardiovascular
disease before their deaths and in my mother's family,
CVD can be traced back at least three generations on
the family tree. Whether because of sudden heart attacks, high
blood pressure, high cholesterol, bypass surgeries or defective

heart valves, our family knows a bit about the disease and its impact. As a child, I never thought much of it. I was small in stature with skinny legs and 'knocked knees'. Childhood obesity was not a concern and I was too young and ignorant to health issues to care. I recall my maternal grandmother being ill during my childhood. She was restricted from even moderate exertion or work by her physician, so she spent most of her time baking, working in her garden or resting.

As a physician, my father encouraged my siblings and me to take good care of ourselves and to be mindful of our physical and mental health. Both my siblings studied sciences (my sister is a physician and my brother is a chemical engineer) so appreciation of biological sciences is natural for them. I on the other hand studied business and labor relations so my appreciation of biological sciences was rooted in a desire to be healthy, not advanced learning. My comprehensive appreciation of my father's lessons didn't occur until I became a parent. It was then that I finally realized I needed to be healthy for myself, but to also teach my children how to be healthy. As a parent,

············✦············

As gifts from God, our children must not only be taught but nurtured, and care of the heart is spiritual as well as physical. It was this deeper understanding of my role as a parent that caused me to go to great lengths to break the cycle of heart disease in our family by teaching our children how to eat well, exercise, and avoid or at least manage stress.

············✦············

I came to realize that good parenting involves more than being the traditional role model, rule-setter, and provider for your children. Parenting requires good and comprehensive stewardship of a child. As gifts from God, our children must not only be taught but nurtured, and care of the heart is spiritual as well as physical. It was this deeper understanding of my role as a parent that caused me to go to great lengths to break the cycle of heart disease in our family by teaching our children how to eat well, exercise, and avoid or at least manage stress.

In addition, a very close childhood friend suffered from heart disease and actually died while waiting for a hospital admission for cardiac services. She and all of her siblings except one have died. As I reflected on her situation, I was compelled to do some homework, research the situation, and better educate myself about cardiovascular disease. Statistically, the disease is the leading cause of death amongst African American women. It exceeds the incident of death due to other major illnesses and diseases including all forms of cancer.

The data warranted aggressive education and prevention measures within the community but target marketing on this issue was not visible in my community.

After seeking assistance from the local hospital and other health outlets, I discussed the issue with a few friends and colleagues. At the time, I didn't fully understand that most of the high-visibility advocacy and fundraising primarily benefited research, development and administration of volunteer offices. What I did understand was that many women of color in my community were either sick or suffering from some form of the disease. Therefore we decided to target low to moderate-income women for our advocacy and education campaign.

For nine years, a public education and awareness campaign was promoted in the community. It was my small way of convincing my employer and community supporters to help educate women to be more proactive about their health. Lower income women were more susceptible to the disease because of limited income, poor eating habits, stress and lower priority for obtaining preventive health care. We named the campaign "*From Our Hearts to Yours*" and provided a lunchtime lecture and a heart-healthy meal. Corporate and community sponsors supported the campaign. My greatest support came from administrators with the University of North Carolina at Wilmington's then School of Nursing (Dr. Betty Glenn and Dr. Virginia Adams). A local jeweler and his wife provided support by partnering with us and through limited independent funds that our agency raised, they enabled us to purchase and provide gifts for program participants. The idea was to not only educate, but for the event to give every woman in attendance a nice gift to remind her to take care of herself. After his death, his wife Janice continued to support our initiative and encouraged me to continue the work at hand. Kingoff's Jewelers proved to not only be a business but a business with owners who care about the community in more ways than one.

Medical professionals traveled to Wilmington to speak with our participants and to help with education and advocacy. In 2007, I was nominated for General Mills Corporation's *Sisters Saving Hearts* award. The program was a national initiative by General Mills to recognize five women around the country for their work in cardiovascular disease awareness and education. Unbelievably, I was one of the 2007 winners. The $5,000 mini-grant that I received was donated to my employer to help us continue the campaign since we were not approved to use government funding for the initiative.

By 2010, we planned and coordinated a benefit concert *"Heart Strings, Music for the Soul"* with the objective of raising funds to help elderly low-income women with food and medicine purchases. The event was hosted by my church and various genres of soothing music were performed by community youth, the Fayetteville State University Choir, jazz artists and members of the Wilmington Symphony Orchestra. The link between cardiovascular health, spirituality and stress reduction was the theme of the event.

The average annual household income for the targeted women was just a few hundred dollars over government guidelines for receiving assistance, yet many were malnourished or cutting their medicine in half to make it stretch until they could afford their next refills. They epitomized the plight of low-income seniors faced with choosing medicine or food in an era of government cutbacks and conflicting regulations on how individuals qualify for assistance. The project was successful, and through nominations from local churches, more than 25 women received assistance that year in the form of gift cards to purchase groceries or medicine. The number of women assisted seemed small, but the impact was great. While we were educating these women on how to be healthier, they received a brief reprieve from the financial burdens that limited the quality of their lives. It was gratifying although we fell under sharp criticism by our state funding source and some in the community who did not support the cause. Our largest funder applauded our efforts and in a monitoring report, deemed the program a strength of the organization in which I was employed.

Determined to continue, I continued to reached out for unconventional support from corporations, businesses and other nonprofit organizations that supported the campaign. To spread the spirit of advocacy and education, we also engaged local churches in a campaign that we named "Bless Her Heart Sunday". Local churches were asked to encourage their congregations to wear red on the second Sunday in February. It was a simple, no cost way of making a statement, and through support from the American Heart Association we provided educational materials for inclusion in Sunday bulletins. Our hope and prayer was that people would read, become proactive, and take charge of their health by getting a check-up. Over the years of CVD education and advocacy, I realized that my friend and her siblings might have lived longer lives if they had received some of the education and support that our campaign offered.

I recall receiving feedback one year from a staff member after one of our largest events. She stated that some members of our team did not like the program because it targeted minority women, and they felt forced to participate. Yet, those women constituted more than 90% of our customer base and no woman was excluded because of race, creed, color, etc. I was disheartened and confused that the human spirit would be so selfish and uncaring about women who needed our aid.

By 2012, I was contacted and offered an opportunity to be interviewed on public television (UNC-TV) with one of our past guest speakers and advocates – Dr. Brenda Armstrong of Duke University Medical Center. I was honored and humbled although weary of the politics and social fights that became necessary to keep the program alive. Board members in my organization were excited, almost ecstatic in the early days of the program. However the program staff and I received marginal assistance from our board as the program continued. Only a few individual board members "stepped up" to continue the effort. The positive publicity and corporate mini-grant fueled the excitement, but in time, the enthusiasm waned. Yet, following our eighth year, participant surveys suggested that the advocacy and education made a difference for a majority of our event participants. Within my community, our strongest support came from the Links, Incorporated, an international organization of women of color devoted to improving their communities.

When I left the agency, my husband and I decided to establish a small foundation to continue the work. Whether the idea was popular or not, the statistics indicated there was still a need. Until the CVD deaths in the community began to decrease, there was still work to be done.

Scripture teaches us through Old Testament lessons that destruction occurs through a lack of knowledge and that a lack of vision adversely affects potential for prosperity. Saving hearts became a lifelong commitment both for my heart and the hearts of other women. Without healthy physical hearts we cannot live and we cannot stave off other diseases that may invade our bodies. Without healthy hearts, we are doomed to early deaths. And without healthy spiritual hearts, we do not realize our full potential and productively engage with other souls on this journey. This work transformed my soul; this work transformed my heart.

"My people are destroyed for lack of knowledge…"
(Hosea 4:6)

Reflections
How do you strive to be physically healthier?
Do you use these techniques just to help yourself,
or do you spread the good news to others in
hopes of helping them to be healthier?
What patterns of disease exist on your family
tree that might be prevented through better
education and proactive health practices?
How do you feel saving lives will help you to grow
spiritually, rather than focusing only on your own life?

"Consider it all joy, my brethren, when you encounter various trials, knowing that the testing of your faith produces endurance. And let endurance have its perfect result, so that you may be perfect and complete, lacking in nothing."
(James 1:2-4,NASB)

Bloodied but Unbowed

For more than 35 years, I devoted my professional work life to developing a well-rounded career. My goals were not lofty but the idea of working in the same place for 35 or 40 years did not appeal to me at all. I had friends who believed that was the path to security. I didn't agree. I wanted to develop my skills as a human resource professional in different venues – corporate, higher education, government and ultimately to bring my knowledge to the nonprofit world. Aside from the years and money invested in a college education, I was a working mother and it was natural for me to apply all that I learned in school, use it to be a helpmate to my husband and to experience the gratification that a healthy career provides. The first 20 years of my career were spent primarily in higher education administration, private industry (telecommunications) and municipal government. My original career development plan seemed to work. The logic in doing so was to be successful and marketable as a human resource professional in *any* business setting.

When I ultimately left my last human resource management post, it was not to move on to the next setting. Instead, it was to seek out a completely new profession. I was burning out, though very successful by career standards. I wanted to give more to help others and didn't feel that my work was making enough of a positive impact on people.

A brief time after attempting to make the career shift, I was approached by a community leader and asked to apply for a position with a nonprofit organization. My first reaction was a firm "No". However after some consideration, I decided to apply. Despite some resistance from one member of the governing board, I was voted into the position after a long and arduous search and screening process. Maslow's Hierarchy of Needs would define this as my moment of self-autonomy. However, the environment that I found myself in was much like the relationship between the legislative, judicial and executive branches of the federal government. When each branch does not work together for the common good, you have problems.

I was hired to be a change agent during a time when the organization was in turmoil. Everything that I knew about management and employee relations was put to the test. Days were long, and some nights were sleepless. However, within my first three years the organization improved its status with stakeholders and we embarked on a path to reach excellence. Despite ongoing self-assessments and an ever-changing service environment, we marched forward with new and innovative approaches to serving those in need. We met with a great deal of success on many fronts.

By my tenth year in the organization, I was beginning to feel the tug of change. Not just change needed in the organization, but personal changes that I needed to make. As in any situation our operating environment was changing. Stakeholders' requirements were rapidly changing, needs of our customers were changing, and the need for new approaches to old social problems was inherent.

The effort to keep pace on all fronts mimicked a large ship attempting to make a sharp turn in the ocean without reducing speed. It was devastating and a very physically and emotionally draining time in my life. In another book I explore in detail the politics of serving the underprivileged community. I took responsibility for the helm as captain of our ship, but many to whom I reported didn't assert their skills and talents to minimize the challenges and help us to successfully sail forward. Instead, they began to step away. A dear friend and colleague advised me to "jump ship" and leave while I was "on top". If my work had been self-serving, that would've been the thing to do. But it was at that turbulent point in time that I realized true servant-leadership is not about the leader. It is instead about those you are serving. So I stayed, trying to make all pieces of the agency's service delivery puzzle fit. I stayed in an effort to be conduit between the organization and its stakeholders.

It was the most difficult time of my career. Before passing away, my father advised me to 'just bail'. Being an Air Force veteran, he likened my situation to an airplane in trouble and limited crew to help keep it in the air. Jet fighters were shooting at us every step of the way, even those fighters that seemingly were on our side. I didn't take his advice because of my commitment to the organization and the people that it served. However, it was probably one of my greatest regrets only because a daughter always strives to follow her father's advice and I didn't take some of the last advice my father gave me. The stakes were high – but my commitment to the children and families that we served was higher.

Ultimately, the organization faltered and lost funding. I was grateful for the very few staff members who understood the bigger picture and stayed on when they could have quit. Swallowing all of my pride, I continued the paper chase and close out of work that stakeholders required. Many colleagues and acquaintances wondered how and why I continued. They didn't realize that the same stakeholders that lost faith in the organization later realized it wasn't my office that failed, but the system that failed. I was asked to stay behind and properly close things out and became the conduit between the governing body of the organization and its stakeholders.

My family thought I was crazy. In the words of a former supervisor, my stock had dropped, lower than the 1929 Wall

Street crash. Only my faith, my family and God sustained me. Jesus walked with me and talked with me and kept me through it all. I reached a point where I didn't want to deal with the public; not in organizations, not even in my church. Too many people didn't know all of the facts, and as human nature goes, too many opinions were being formed. For those who could have aided the organization but chose to jump ship, I lost a great deal of any respect I may have previously held for them. For those who decided to go the distance, I simply felt a lot of gratitude. Deep down, I knew I had an obligation to complete the job with grace and professionalism but it was difficult.

I found my doctors to be an unexpected but wonderful source of support. When time came for annual physicals, mammograms and other routine tests, it was refreshing to hear comments about their knowledge of my professional woes, and the words of encouragement they offered me. One physician offered to send my resume to his sister to help me make a career change. I thought he was just joking but on a follow up visit, he assured me he wasn't. Despite all I had been taught by my father about building a relationship with health care providers, I believed that on most days I was just another file number. It was when I arrived at an office, went into the examining room or the doctor's private office for consultation that I realized I had connected with not only excellent practitioners but caring professionals. They helped guide my soul while keeping my body healthy. My father's firm advice about carefully selecting your healthcare provider paid off. It's always a combination of competence and compassion. Knowing that you're not just a number to someone who has so much control over your ability to live a longer and healthier life is an assuring feeling.

Once my work was completed, I realized it was time to go – not when the 'going was tough' – but instead, when the work was done. There were occasions when I would see some former staff and customers with their children. Their kind words and expressions of gratitude confirmed that I did facilitate many works that helped people in my community. It was well with my soul.

My governing body however, continued to reach out to me for assistance after my departure. Politely, and in a volunteer mode, I continued to help them. I found it extremely interesting that so many of the things I attempted to guide or advise them on in the past, and that were ignored, were suddenly important. My confirmation of what went wrong in that organization was received, and it wasn't me. My head was bloodied, but unbowed. My faith and my God had brought me through an excruciatingly painful episode in my career. Ironically, it was my true season of servanthood that brought the most pain and challenge in my career. Yet, Jesus brought me peace like a river. Despite the advice of many, I let go at the right time. I had to be reminded that my faith would be tried for a reason. My soul was transformed and as my grandfather would say many years ago, "what didn't kill my spirit made me stronger".

In the fell clutch of circumstance I have
not winced nor cried aloud.
Under the bludgeonings of chance my
head is bloody, but unbowed.

Reflections

What life experience(s) have made you question just
how far you could go in accomplishing a task?
What did you do to preserve the spirit
of service in your work?
Where did you find solace and peace
during challenging moments?
What would you do differently?

Part III
Transformations and the Road Ahead

Coffee, Tea and the Family Tree

Bless the Lord o' my soul
For the faint whispers in my ear from times of old.
Bless the Lord, o' my soul for the family history,
Passed down, and responsibly told.

I n many families, the tradition of passing history forward is a primary responsibility of the eldest in each generation. While this is not always the case, it is a southern tradition. It is also an African tradition and it is a tradition within my family. Many generations ago, when reading or writing by people of African descent was not permitted, the tradition of passing oral history down in the family was necessary to ensure that each generation to come would know and understand its roots.

A Morning Cup of Coffee

As a child, I have fond memories of waking up to the aroma of freshly brewed coffee. It was a staple in our household and always signaled the beginning of my mother's day. Coffee was not consumed throughout the day or in the evenings unless a pot was brewed to accompany a special homemade dessert such as my grandmother's pineapple-coconut layer cake. No, coffee was the staple that started the adults in our home on their way each day. For me, it brought an aroma that signaled time to get up and get ready for school. I do not remember a day in my childhood when I did not awaken to the smell of freshly brewed coffee.

As time passed and I grew to my teen years, coffee became a beverage that I could have a "sip" of. The idea that it was ok for a child to have coffee in any form (including today's iced coffee beverages) was unacceptable. My brother and I enjoyed our morning cup of juice or milk instead. However, as I began my preparation to transition from high school to college, my mother found opportunities to introduce me gradually to her freshly brewed coffee. A most important point was that "instant" coffee was not the preferred beverage. If freshly brewed coffee wasn't available, then instant was ok for the sake of having a bit of caffeine to get my day started. Second, coffee was consumed black with only a little sugar. Milk or cream was an acceptable additive, but it masked the true flavor of a good blend of coffee. It was therefore important to select a good brand, have the coffee beans ground just right, and always make sure the coffee was fresh.

I found in the days to come that I would apply my mother's formula for good coffee to many life situations. It was always necessary to select the best. Why settle for less than the best and compromise on the taste and satisfaction of consuming a good cup of coffee? Also, not to dilute the brew. If it's too strong, why mask it with sweeteners or flavor enhancements? Just select the right blend, brew it properly, get it right, and enjoy! This principle would be applied to many of the choices I made in life, and many of the experiences I would come to enjoy.

An Afternoon Cup of Tea

After living in the midwest for many years, I returned to my Southern hometown in 1993. My mother passed suddenly from a massive heart attack and old tugs to return south had resurfaced in my soul. What appeared to be a relatively easy transition of my family from Illinois to North Carolina proved to be more difficult than I expected and a few months into the first phase of our move, I was feeling weary living out of suitcases and boxes.

One spring afternoon, I received a call from my fifth grade teacher – Mrs. Mamie Harris. She called to invite me over to a friend's home for lunch. Mrs. Harris was always a very kind and gentle, yet demanding teacher and I was so happy that she thought enough of me upon my return home to reach out. Yet, the idea of lunch at a friend's home was a bit puzzling. Nevertheless, I accepted the invitation.

On the day of our luncheon date, I didn't quite know what to expect. Her friend was someone I knew only from a distant memory in my childhood. She was also a retired teacher but not a very familiar face or name that I grew up with. Mrs. Harris' home would have been just fine for lunch but I thought "Oh well, I'll sign out for a slightly longer lunch hour and enjoy the moment".

Upon my arrival I was pleasantly surprised by the setting. Much to my surprise I was greeted not only by Mrs. Harris, but a few other retired educators and a couple of women whom I'd never met. The soup and sandwich luncheon that I expected was instead a bit of a tea party. Nicely arranged card tables were neatly dressed with crisp white table linens and decorated with little centerpieces. Assorted salads, glasses of iced-tea and scrumptious southern pound cake slices awaited us all. A young man, whose parents I would soon develop an acquaintance with, was in the sunroom playing a violin. My brain said "what's going on here?". My soul answered, "Sit back, relax and be a good student".

The occasion was flattering to say the very least but before I would allow my ego to get the best of me, I had to ask Mrs. Harris why the southern formalities. With an enchanting smile and twinkle in her eyes, she whispered to me, "we want you to get to know us, and know more about who you are." Her response caused a slight uneasiness within me because I didn't understand how these women would help me to know more about myself. I egotistically thought *"I know who I am"*. After lunchtime conversation about my job, my move back to North Carolina and my family, we recessed to the living room for coffee, tea and dessert.

It was over the familiar beverage from my childhood memories that one by one, the women wove a missing piece of my family's tapestry. As I listened to their stories, I recalled persons who seemingly watched over me as a child – Nada Cotton – the librarian at Wilmington's "colored library" and Mamie Harris – my fifth grade teacher who demanded excellence, amongst many others. Not only were they guardian angels but family members from an injured and slightly detached branch on our family tree. There were others who explained why during the early years of school desegregation in our town, my mother opposed my father's wishes to send me to the "white" elementary schools that some children were enrolled in as integration of schools occurred. In her mind, and the minds of the women present that day, it was more important for me to continue in a "safe" zone – schools that would ground me in my community, and in my knowledge of who I was as an African-American child. It was an insightful moment to sit and listen as these women poured out their wisdom upon me, transforming my views and opinions of them from childhood memories to adult perspectives.

A lone voice in the group softly said "I have a gift for you." I did not know this woman and her face was not at all familiar. She handed me a booklet, 8.5 x 11 in size and spiral bound with a black spine. I did not know what it was nor what to expect. As I proceeded to turn it over, she said, "my name is Myrtle Stackhouse, and we have the same family roots." The cover of the booklet read *A History of the Howe Family.*

Myrtle Stackhouse was a distant cousin on the family tree. The Howe family roots that my father and his grandmother so often spoke of were confirmed that day by her. Many family secrets and threads to our family tapestry that were never fully explained to me as a child were made crystal clear that day by elder females in my paternal family tree. Her little booklet closed a significant patch in the tapestry of my father's family. Leaves on the tree that always appeared to be just shadows began to shine brightly in the sunlight as the winds tossed the tree branches and exposed the beautiful hidden leaves. I suddenly understood the days when teachers, librarians or church members would ask about my report card, or if I was having difficulty with a subject and needed help in school. They were quiet guardians watching over me during my childhood and upon my return home, they decided that it was time to make sure the information that they held was passed forward. That afternoon also enlightened me about the impact that the 1898 Racial Massacre had on families of African descent in my hometown. Information that was not openly discussed about Wilmington's past was quietly kept and held by family historians. I was grateful that the questions I asked in a public library over 25 years earlier were finally answered for me by members of my family. It would be another five years before the 100 year commemoration of the event would occur, but my experience that afternoon made me feel I was ahead of the curve in so many ways.

I will always remember that day. There were other days when my mother told me the railroad stories of her father's day, or the plantation stories of her grandmother's era. My husband's grandmother would tell me her family's history in Arkansas back to the revolutionary war, and upon the birth of our son Phillip, Jr., she wrote by hand those same stories for me to pass to him and all of our children.

It was on such days and during such times that my soul was further transformed. I came to realize as an adult that without a tightly woven tapestry, we don't understand the fabric of our families, and we therefore can't understand the fabric of our own lives. When we are fortunate enough to know our roots, know ourselves, and pass our history forward to the next generation, we empower our next generation to travel the road ahead with self-esteem, self-confidence and a formula for success.

A Glimpse into the Past &
A Vision for the Future

In 1898, Wilmington, N.C. was the site of an incident that has been labeled as the only coup d'état in American history. Driven by the winds of post-Reconstruction Era politics, people of African descent were killed, run out of town or otherwise intimidated to rob them of authority, power and personal property. My father's grandmother was 12 years old and an eye-witness to the incident. Along with her mother and other women and children, she hid in Pine Forest cemetery (a cemetery for people of color) for safety and shelter on the first night of the violence. The incident left a deep scar on Wilmington and especially those remaining residents of African descent.

My great-grandmother died while I was still a young child. When her health began to fail, her daughter (my grandmother) took her to Pennsylvania to live with her. Before she passed away, my parents arranged for us to visit with her. I vividly recall seeing her lying in bed rambling about things I did not understood. In her ramblings, she grabbed my wrist and said, "don't let them do this again… make sure to hide if they do". I remember feeling very frightened. I had no clue of what she was talking about. In frustration, my father instructed my mother to remove me and my brother from the room out of his concern that his grandmother was frightening us. As my mother pulled me away, I felt as though I was in a tug-of-war because my grandma Thalia wouldn't let go of my arm. She kept babbling and when she did let go, she quietly said "don't forget". I will always remember her face when she uttered those last words to me. It took a decade for me to begin to understand the message she was trying to communicate to me.

As a teenager in high school, my friend Carr and I made a trip to the main library. We heard tidbits of information about the 1898 Massacre but it was never discussed in school. Only during my teen years did my mother begin to tell me what she knew about it. Her parents came to Wilmington after the turn of the century so the information was not handed down in the Sutton/Thompson family tree. It was passed down in the Howe family tree – my father's family. The visit to the main branch of the public library was our commitment to go and find out what secrets had been hidden for so long. Our trip was unsuccessful. We did not receive any assistance in researching information that we were told was "in the vault". I left for college vowing to someday piece together the missing information that my great-grandmother Thalia wanted me to have. As a young woman, my father wrote letters to me, enclosing copies of family information and documents that had been entrusted to him.

At the time, I lived away from Wilmington in a different state but upon my mother's death decided to return home. I had a burning desire to return to my Southern roots with a hope of somehow "giving back" to the community that I emerged from. When he declared me the family historian, he decided that I was old enough and spiritually mature enough to manage the information that he imparted upon me. The raw truth about the incident was overwhelming.

For years, the incident was not openly discussed until community organizers and leaders planned and executed a centennial commemoration of the event. It was quite successful and was followed by the erection of a public memorial to the victims, the opening of a public dialogue to begin a healing process, and numerous books and writings that were published. In the process, many family documents and a great deal of hidden history were illuminated.

Reflecting on my great-grandmother's life, she remained in Wilmington after the incident. As a young woman, she went into domestic service and began raising her own family, later assisting with her grandchildren. She worked for many years as a cook for the Parsley family on Masonboro Sound. Over time, my father would come to share wonderful stories about his grandmother's cooking, his love of seafood from the sound, and the few occasions on which he was allowed to visit the Parsley residence on Masonboro known as Live Oaks.

When I returned to Wilmington in 1993, I decided to feed my appetite for local history. I began by assisting and later being appointed to the Pine Forest Cemetery Board of Trustees. Pine

Forest was and always will be dear to my heart, for it provided shelter and safety on a night when my great-grandmother could have been killed. Her death at the tender age of 12 would have altered the DNA of our family tree. Her daughter, my father, nor I, as I am, never would have been born. I therefore felt an obligation to the grand lady called Pine Forest. Pine Forest also held the remains of my great-grandmother's ancestors and my mother's parents. As a child, we were taught the holiday ritual of going to Pine Forest on Easter, Memorial Day, Mother's Day, Father's Day, Veteran's Day and Christmas morning to visit family gravesites and place fresh flowers. This ritual would be passed on to my children. Now they all live in other cities except our youngest son. But even today, when I am caught in the kitchen panicked about holiday dinner being served on time, it is our son Phillip who reminds me to take the drive to Pine Forest before the day gets away from us to place flowers on gravesites.

I later served briefly on the Historic Wilmington Foundation's Board of Directors. I wanted to dive into the work of the board, but the job that I held made it difficult to carve out time for rest and relaxation, not to mention volunteerism. I ultimately withdrew from service on the board, but had the opportunity to work with its director for a brief time. We shared many concerns and engaged in meaningful conversations about historic preservation and especially the history of the African American community in Wilmington.

In 2010, the Foundation's annual black tie fundraiser was planned and would be held at Live Oaks on Masonboro

Sound. There was a part of me that didn't want to attend. The remembrance of my father's stories about his grandmother, though positive, left an uneasy feeling in my soul. I had mixed emotions about going there but an inner voice spoke to me saying "Go".

On the day of the event, my husband developed a hacking cough and fever. It was a particularly cool autumn, and it was clear that he didn't need to be out in the evening air. I really didn't want to attend alone, and called my father to say I was considering not going. After all, my tickets were purchased and I had fulfilled a portion of my obligation as a board member. But after talking with him, that nagging feeling returned and the voice inside me again said "GO". My father was suffering from a myriad of health issues and could no longer travel. Stories from home were of interest to him, and accordingly he kept up with my community service and involvement. He insisted that I attend and report to him on every moment of the evening. So I asked our son Phillip to attend with me. He was a college student studying creative writing at the time and I decided this might be a good experience for him.

There is a great deal of history on Masonboro Sound and I wanted him to see it. Local records document the history of Live Oaks. The residence was designed by Henry Bacon (architect and designer of the Lincoln Memorial in Washington, D.C.) for Walter Linton Parsley and his wife Agnes MacRae Parsley. It is a beautiful meeting of the water and the land, graced by stately oak and southern magnolia trees that tower over the man-made architecture. The estate is home to Sarah Parsley, widow of

Walter Linton Parsley's grandson, Walter. I wanted my son to see and experience the beauty of Live Oaks.

Fortunately, he and his father were the same suit size so we decided he would wear his father's tuxedo. My son renewed my interest in attending as I talked with him on the drive across the county to Masonboro Sound. I suddenly realized that fate had presented a perfect opportunity to continue the oral tradition of passing history from one generation to another in the family.

The night was cool, and the gala was held under a tent pitched on the grounds of the residence. I did not initially realize it but there was a full moon hovering above us with a beautiful halo adorning it. After being greeted by Mrs. Parsley inside her home and speaking with guests, my son Phillip and I took a stroll away from the tent towards the water. It was a very surreal moment and we stood there for what seemed like an hour talking about families, the past, and how it impacts the present. I was happy for my years spent in Chicago, for what was considered a real chilly night by Southern standards was comfortable for us. It also allowed us to have the stretch of the grounds to ourselves while most of the guests stayed under the tent. We later returned to the party, had dinner, fellowshipped with others, participated in the silent auction that benefited the foundation, took photos and in general, enjoyed the evening.

I left the Parsley residence that night less concerned about the fact that my great-grandmother Thalia was once the family cook. It was more important to me that roughly 100 years later, her great-granddaughter and a great-great grandson (whom she never lived to meet) could be on the guest list for a fundraiser at the residence. In spite of all the work still to be done in society, progress has been made. Definitely not enough, but progress has occurred. Telling a part of the family history to my son, and in the place where it occurred made the history lesson more relevant and better appreciated. There were other places we would visit, in neighboring Sampson County and other parts of New Hanover County, continuing the oral tradition within our family.

In the spirit, I felt my great-grandma Thalia's presence that night. I had received an opportunity to visit a chapter in my family's past and to take my son with me. My parents always taught me that you must know your history to understand where you're going (or possibly where you don't want to go back to). On this occasion, I was able to help him see the relevance of his past to the present, and to look beyond the present to the unlimited potential of the future. My soul was lifted, and I had a divine assurance that the legacy of documenting, preserving and telling our family's history would not be lost to the winds of time. That evening, one of our children paused to look back with me and to set his compass for a good course into the future.

I was reminded of the responsibility we all have to know ourselves, our past, and our present. With that knowledge we can confidently stand in the present, boldly walk into the future, and responsibly build our children's self-esteem in the knowledge of who they are. This not only transforms our souls but shapes the souls of our next generation.

Reflections

What legacy do you wish to leave your family?
What efforts have been made to record
and preserve your family's history?
How do you make the tradition of passing history on to
younger family members relevant and interesting?

Care for Your Garden and Increase Your Blossoms

Blossom \'blä-səm\ *n*...**1a**: the flower of a seed plant; also: the mass of such flowers on a single plant **b**: the state of bearing flowers **2**: a peak period or stage of development (Merriam-Webster's Collegiate Dictionary – Eleventh Edition)

B utterflies flutter gracefully in gardens filled with beautiful, vibrant flowers. The right flowers whose stems are filled with abundant blossoms provide the nourishing nectar that butterflies need. Not only do they need nectar for nourishment, they thrive on nectar from the right flowers.

Throughout various stages of life, I have found myself walking through different gardens. Some were fertile and full of life with deep rooted plants bearing beautiful and fragrant flowers. Others have been colorful and full of plants, but when I walked closely amongst the garden's inhabitants, the sweet fragrance of life was not there. I have even found myself surrounded by beautiful blossoms that stunk when I placed my nose close to the flower to enjoy its fragrance.

As with all things, we must take care of the garden in which our souls live, to ensure that it is healthy, it is fragrant and that it attracts those people and things that will help us in our growth. The health of our garden is determined by condition of the soil. As in the parable of the planter as written in the Gospel of Matthew, when seeds are sown in the garden of life, we must take care to sow our seeds on good, fertile ground. We must remove the rocks from the soil so that the seeds can take root and grow deep roots to withstand windy days, drought and stormy seasons. I have often advised our daughter of the difference in friends and acquaintances, cautioning her that friends have deeper roots than those individuals who stand with you only on sunny days and for superficial reasons. Friends stand when storms come, and bask in the bright light of sunny days with you. They never attempt to overshadow or dominate but to compliment and support.

Fertile ground will not only grow beautiful plants but will provide nourishment for the weeds that will appear in the garden. Weeds are sometimes distinct in their appearance, but can sometimes mimic the appearance of a flower or flowering plant. Therefore the good gardener must be vigilant and watchful as the garden grows, for some weeds can grow alongside good plants, working deception in our souls and manifesting its deception through confusion. If not careful they can be harvested and consumed through sight, smell or digestion, polluting our souls. But a good gardener will harvest all before consuming, sorting the weeds from the flowers before consumption. How often we mistakenly engage with, dance around, or otherwise consume the weeds of life instead of the flowers – all because of deception.

The care and nurturing of our gardens will bring forth bright and beautiful blossoms to be enjoyed in life - blossoms that yield the fruit of the spirit, manifested in those around us and manifested in our thoughts, words and deeds. You will know them as blossoms of love, joy, peace, patience, kindness, goodness, faithfulness, gentleness and self-control.

I am thankful for the presence of Jesus in my life, for all the days of my life, now, before and whatever days are yet to come. In the garden, he has walked and talked with me, and given me a keen sense of the flowers versus the weeds. It is a relationship that I had to grow up to as my soul transformed.

And it is a critical relationship that we must all have with Him to avoid the deceptive snares that can be found in the most beautiful of gardens. The divine discernment that I have experienced when no logic or tangible explanation could be given to a situation is something that can only be received from God. Once you experience it, you will never forget it; once you experience it, you know that your soul has been transformed.

The divine discernment
that I have experienced
when no logic or tangible
explanation could be
given to a situation is
something that can only
be received from God.
Once you experience it,
you will never forget it;
once you experience it,
you know that your soul
has been transformed.

A Welcomed Transition

"For I am now ready to be offered, and the time of my
departure is at hand. I have fought a good fight, I have
finished my course, I have kept the faith: Henceforth there
is laid up for me a crown of righteousness, which the Lord,
the righteous judge, shall give me at that day: and not to
me only, but unto all them also that love his appearing."
(2 Timothy 4:6-8)

Too often we confuse the phenomenon known as death
in our grammatical reference to it. Not to be mistaken
as a *place*, death is the *vehicle* by which we make our
passage to the next dimension of life. It is a conductor that is
feared and dreaded by many, but welcomed by so many others.
Psalm 23 teaches us that even when we walk through the valley
of the shadow of death, we should fear no evil. I believe that no
one wants to let go of the earthly attachments we develop. It is
a very human trait that we possess. Love for one another, love
of our children and families, love of the beauty of the earth that
surrounds us, and love of the things we possess while we walk

> For the believer, life must be lived to its fullest and we must live in Christ, for we know not the hour or the day when our life's work will be deemed complete.

the earth all keep our souls heavy and bound to our earthly existence. Yet those who believe in Christ as their savior, and keep their trust and faith in Him, die without fear of what lies beyond. They die without fear for what or who they will leave behind. They know that without the act of physically declining and dying, our souls are not released from the earthly vessels containing us, and we would be unable to return to our true spiritual home. For the believer, life must be lived to its fullest and we must live in Christ, for we know not the hour or the day when our life's work will be deemed complete. Whenever it is determined that our work here is done, it is only the assurance that we have done all that we could, and that we did what we could to God's glory, that gives us the confidence to move on, to go forward and to physically die in order to live to the utmost, in spirit.

I have experienced the visitation of death upon family, friends and colleagues. It has come with expectation and it has come completely unexpected. I have watched loved ones suffer and decline in physical health for extended periods of time and I have experienced loved ones die without notice. For those who believed in Christ and expected death's early arrival in their lives, the peace that exuded from them surpassed any understanding that I could have had.

I learned many lessons about trust, faith and love as I watched two dear friends prepare for death's arrival. While I suffered emotionally watching their decline, they encouraged me to remember that this is not our home. They reminded me that we become so earthbound until we become heavy in ourselves and in doing so, we forget the light and heavenly nature of the spirit that resides in us. I was reminded that love is not selfish, does not stifle, nor grasp with a tight grip. Love instead enjoys, encourages, and embraces to support, not to control. Love recognizes when it is time to let go and will do so when necessary, for the greater good of the soul.

On the highway of divine life, death's destination can turn right or left when we reach the appointed intersection. Where death takes us is a choice that we make; a choice that is made by the life we live and our faith in God through Jesus His son. When death does arrive, the believer has no fear. And those of us left behind should rejoice that another faithful soul has found its way back home. My friends Annie and Jean taught me this wonderful lesson about life. *It is an ultimate metamorphosis of the soul.*

"O death, where is thy sting? O grave, where is thy victory? The sting of death is sin; and the strength of sin is the law. But thanks be to God, which giveth us the victory through our Lord Jesus Christ. Therefore my beloved brethren, be stedfast, unmoveable, always abounding in the work of the Lord, forasmuch as ye know that your labour is not in vain in the Lord."

(I Corinthians 15:55-58)

Epilogue

In the introduction to this book, I reflected on the analogy between our spiritual growth, transformation of the soul, and the life cycle of butterflies. You have taken a glimpse into those people, places and events that have transformed my soul and caused me to grow in my faith. There is more to my life story but my hope was to share a few of the more significant experiences with you, the reader. As we look forward down an untraveled path, I encourage you to remember that while some butterflies and moths resemble each other, they are two distinctly different creatures. Both lack a backbone, but we have Christ as the backbone of our lives, therefore as believers, let us be further distinguished.

Butterflies have a tendency to fly during the daytime while many moths generally are nocturnal and fly at night. Therefore, as Jesus explained to his disciples in John 9:4, work while it is day, for night will come when no one will be able to work. Butterflies have a wing structure that allows them to fly with a lighter and more graceful flight than moths. Moths have a wing structure that causes them to fly more mechanically, almost in a stiff way. Finally, both have antennas but moth antennas are simple and straight. They look like miniature rabbit ears on old televisions. Butterflies instead have long antennas that end like a golf club. In addition to using their antennas for smell, researchers now report that butterflies use their antennas as a type of GPS system, migrating based on the sun and its position in the sky! How marvelous when we navigate through life like the butterfly, setting our compass on the Son and traveling under His direction.

I hope you will let your soul mimic the butterfly. May your flight in life be light and graceful, present while there is still daylight in life, flying high, and always remembering to come down to the nourishing and restoring nectar of the flowers in God's garden. I pray you will allow Him to be your shelter in storms, a place of perfect refuge in the garden. And in your flight, may you grow in Christ, always spiraling upward in your walk of faith, using all of your God-given faculties and talents to absorb and be a part of all that is good in life. Be ever mindful to avoid the danger of deceptions that wait to ensnare you and entrap your soul.

Let your soul be transformed as the butterfly is in its life cycle.

Coming Soon From C. J. Brown
The Politics of Poverty
How Head Start Changed My Life